The Badass BLOG PLANNER

Your guide to defining your purpose, creating clarity, and building a year of killer content

BY SARAH MORGAN

"IT TAKES AS MUCH ENERGY TO WISH AS IT DOES TO PLAN"

- ELEANOR ROOSEVELT

TABLE OF CONTENTS

BADASS BLOG PLANNER

Welcome to the Badass Blog Planner—your ultimate guide for gaining clarity and focus to create brilliant content and grow your online presence over the next 12 months.

Let's be honest, last year, some of us spent way too many nights stressed over post ideas during late-night brainstorming sessions or succumbed to an entire month when blogging felt like the most hated of household chores.

How about we not do that this year? How about we get ahead of the game and make a plan, so blogging feels fresh and exciting? How about we find your blogging tribe and learn what really floats their boat? How about we get super focused and create content that will grow your business by leaps and bounds. And how about we get it all figured out now so you aren't scrambling all year to have a consistent online presence?

Whether you're hoping to grow your readership, increase your sales, or just meet a bunch of spectacular people, looking back on what went well, what totally flopped, and what you'd love to accomplish will help set a course for steady growth year-round!

To accomplish this, we'll figure out what parts of your online strategy make your readers swoon, what's holding you back from mega success, what goals you'd love to conquer, and build a plan to turn you into a content machine.

Focusing on your blog one day at a time will of course get the job done, but having a long-term vision will help bring purpose and pride to what you're creating every day. We want to build one unified brand instead of lots of scattered profiles.

Since I know blogging is only one of the many things on your never-ending to-do list, a year-long plan will help you work smarter, not harder. Bloggers often say making time to write is one of their biggest challenges, so we're going to eliminate that problem by scheduling everything in advance.

You've already got the goods to create content that will entertain, inspire and provide immense value to your readers. So, if you're ready to get serious about growing your brand online, fill out the following worksheets and join me in preparing for a year of smashing internet success!

WHY DO YOU DO WHAT YOU DO?

First up, let's get super clear on what your blog is all about and who you're blogging for.

I blog because . . .

My ideal reader is . . .

I want to help them . . .

I want them to see my blog as . . .

Blogging and social media make me feel good when . . .

BLOG STATS . . .

To track your progress - fill in the date, your current stats, and follower numbers.

Date

Monthly pageviews

Blog subscribers

Email subscribers

Twitter followers

Facebook likes

Pinterest followers

Instagram followers

Youtube subscribers

Google+ followers

Other

ANALYTICS
Google analytics
Analytics.twitter.com
Facebook insights
Instagram: iconosquare.com
Analytics.pinterest.com
youtube.com/analytics

BLOG STATS . . .

LET'S REVIEW

First up, we need to evaluate what went well, what could have gone better, and what was a big fat flop. Since every move you make on your blog or social media affects your brand as a whole, we're going to review every inch of your online presence.

We'll cover content, static pages, social media, projects, products, marketing, advertising, and your overall blog design in order to move forward with clarity and purpose.

Once we have a clear picture of where you stand, we'll create an action plan and set goals to help you become a raging success. *FYI: Because I like to keep everything organized, this year's worksheets are marked in red and next year's plan is in green.*

I did my best to cover every aspect of blogging, but if you didn't do everything included, don't panic! Not all of the worksheets will apply to your blog (they don't all apply to mine either) and that's totally fine. Always do what works best for you, your blog, and your readers!

To help you get started, you may consider creating a survey to find out how your blog looks from your readers' perspective. (I love using Typeform.com for this!) Happy and excited readers will be your best marketing tool as they'll shout from the rooftops and help promote your fantastic content. Here are a few questions to get you going . . .

How often do you read this blog? (daily, weekly, monthly)

How do you read it? (by going to the URL, RSS reader, on my phone, by clicking posts on Twitter/Facebook/Pinterest)

Gender / age / education / marital status / job description

What are your favorite / least favorite categories? (include checkbox lists)

What social media platform do you spend the most time on?

What types of posts do you prefer? (photo-heavy, how-to, personal, etc.)

What do you wish I would write more about?

What can I help you with?

THINGS THAT WERE AWESOME . . .

Oh how we kicked ass this year; let us count the ways! What did you create? Where did you go? Who did you connect with? Big and small—list them all!

THINGS THAT KINDA SUCKED . . .

Did you run into any speed bumps this year? For each item list at least two things you could have done differently to create a better outcome.

CONTENT *(this year)*

Over the past 6 months, which of your posts received the most traffic, comments, and social media engagement? Which posts did you enjoy writing most? Which posts did your readers benefit from the most? Fill out the following three pages and then come back here to record your findings. (You'll find space for a monthly and quarterly content plan starting on page 66)

The types of posts that benefit my readers most are . . .

(long/short, photos, lists, how-to, inspiration, education, entertainment, personal, etc.)

The types of posts I enjoy writing most are . . .

The categories that get the most love are . . .

The day(s) of the week that posts generate the most traffic & shares are . . .

CONTENT *(this year)*

CONTENT...

Post title:

Date posted: Category: Average monthly pageviews:

Comments: Twitter: Facebook: Pinterest:

On a scale of 1-5 how much did you enjoy creating this post?

How did your readers benefit?

- -

Post title:

Date posted: Category: Average monthly pageviews:

Comments: Twitter: Facebook: Pinterest:

On a scale of 1-5 how much did you enjoy creating this post?

How did your readers benefit?

- -

Post title:

Date posted: Category: Average monthly pageviews:

Comments: Twitter: Facebook: Pinterest:

On a scale of 1-5 how much did you enjoy creating this post?

How did your readers benefit?

MORE CONTENT...

Post title:

Date posted: *Category:*   *Average monthly pageviews:*

Comments: *Twitter:*   *Facebook:*   *Pinterest:*

On a scale of 1-5 how much did you enjoy creating this post?

How did your readers benefit?

- -

Post title:

Date posted: *Category:*   *Average monthly pageviews:*

Comments: *Twitter:*   *Facebook:*   *Pinterest:*

On a scale of 1-5 how much did you enjoy creating this post?

How did your readers benefit?

- -

Post title:

Date posted: *Category:*   *Average monthly pageviews:*

Comments: *Twitter:*   *Facebook:*   *Pinterest:*

On a scale of 1-5 how much did you enjoy creating this post?

How did your readers benefit?

MORE CONTENT...

EVEN MORE CONTENT . . .

Post title:

Date posted: Category: Average monthly pageviews:

Comments: Twitter: Facebook: Pinterest:

On a scale of 1-5 how much did you enjoy creating this post?

How did your readers benefit?

- -

Post title:

Date posted: Category: Average monthly pageviews:

Comments: Twitter: Facebook: Pinterest:

On a scale of 1-5 how much did you enjoy creating this post?

How did your readers benefit?

- -

Post title:

Date posted: Category: Average monthly pageviews:

Comments: Twitter: Facebook: Pinterest:

On a scale of 1-5 how much did you enjoy creating this post?

How did your readers benefit?

SOCIAL MEDIA *(this year)*

Social media is the best way to make friends, find clients, build a community, share your expertise, collaborate, promote, and more! Use each platform's analytics to determine what type of content works best to engage your audience and grow your readership.

I use social media to . . .

The top three social media activities that create a worthwhile return are . . .

1.

2.

3.

The best thing I get out of social media is . . .

The most valuable thing I provide my followers on social media is . . .

The platforms that fit best into my daily life are . . .

.

The social media activity that is the biggest pain in the ass is . . .

TWITTER . . .

WHICH OF YOUR TWEETS HAD THE MOST RE-TWEETS + FAVORITES?

For each tweet record the purpose (entertainment, inspiration, education, etc.), the tone (happy, serious, silly), the content (reply, a photo, Twitter chat), along with the day & time.

Tweet:

Day + time:

Purpose:

Tone:

Content: **Re-Tweets:**   **Favorites:**

Tweet:

Day + time:

Purpose:

Tone:

Content: **Re-Tweets:**   **Favorites:**

Tweet:

Day + time:

Purpose:

Tone:

Content: **Re-Tweets:**   **Favorites:**

MORE TWITTER . . .

Tweet:

Day + time:

Purpose:

Tone:

Content: *Re-Tweets:*   *Favorites:*

- -

Tweet:

Day + time:

Purpose:

Tone:

Content: *Re-Tweets:*   *Favorites:*

- -

Tweet:

Day + time:

Purpose:

Tone:

Content: *Re-Tweets:*   *Favorites:*

- -

POPULAR HASHTAGS:

FACEBOOK . . .

WHICH OF YOUR POSTS HAD THE MOST COMMENTS + LIKES?

For each post record the purpose, the content (personal photo, business-oriented, video, link to another resource, etc.), the day and time, and the number of comment and likes.

Post:

Day + time:

Purpose:

Content:

Tags: **Comments:**   **Likes:**

Post:

Day + time:

Purpose:

Content:

Tags: **Comments:**   **Likes:**

Post:

Day + time:

Purpose:

Content:

Tags: **Comments:**   **Likes:**

FACEBOOK . . .

MORE FACEBOOK . . .

Post:

Day + time:

Purpose:

Content:

Tags: *Comments:*   *Likes:*

Post:

Day + time:

Purpose:

Content:

Tags: *Comments:*   *Likes:*

Post:

Day + time:

Purpose:

Content:

Tags: *Comments:*   *Likes:*

NOTES:

MORE FACEBOOK . . .

INSTAGRAM . . .

WHICH OF YOUR PHOTOS HAD THE MOST COMMENTS + LIKES?

For each photo record the caption and tags (people/hashtags), the purpose, the tone, along with the number of comments and likes.

Photo of:

Caption + tags:

Purpose:

Tone:

Comments: **Likes:**

Photo of:

Caption + tags:

Purpose:

Tone:

Comments: **Likes:**

Photo of:

Caption + tags:

Purpose:

Tone:

Comments: **Likes:**

MORE INSTAGRAM . . .

Photo of:

Caption + tags:

Purpose:

Tone:

Comments: *Likes:*

Photo of:

Caption + tags:

Purpose:

Tone:

Comments: *Likes:*

Photo of:

Caption + tags:

Purpose:

Tone:

Comments: *Likes:*

POPULAR HASHTAGS:

FIRST THEY'LL ASK WHY YOU'RE DOING IT . . . LATER THEY'LL ASK HOW YOU DID IT

PINTEREST . . .

WHICH OF YOUR PINS HAD THE MOST ENGAGEMENT + RE-PINS?

For each image pinned from your blog, record the purpose, the content, the boards it was pinned to (note if it was a solo or group board), and the number of re-pins.

Pin:

Purpose:

Content:

Pinned to:

Re-pins:

Pin:

Purpose:

Content:

Pinned to:

Re-pins:

Pin:

Purpose:

Content:

Pinned to:

Re-pins:

MORE PINTEREST . . .

Pin:

Purpose:

Content:

Pinned to:

Re-pins:

Pin:

Purpose:

Content:

Pinned to:

Re-pins:

Pin:

Purpose:

Content:

Pinned to:

Re-pins:

POPULAR HASHTAGS:

YOUTUBE...

WHICH OF YOUR VIDEOS GOT THE MOST LOVE?

For each video, record the purpose, the content, the day and time posted, along with the number of comments and likes.

Video:

Purpose:

Content:

Day + time:

Comments: *Likes:*

Video:

Purpose:

Content:

Day + time:

Comments: *Likes:*

Video:

Purpose:

Content:

Day + time:

Comments: *Likes:*

MORE YOUTUBE . . .

Video:

Purpose:

Content:

Day + time:

Comments: *Likes:*

Video:

Purpose:

Content:

Day + time:

Comments: *Likes:*

Video:

Purpose:

Content:

Day + time:

Comments: *Likes:*

NOTES:

SOCIAL MEDIA *(next year)*

TWITTER

The types of posts followers respond to most are . . .

The best days and times to post are . . .

The tone and content followers benefit from most are . . .

FACEBOOK

The types of posts followers respond to most are . . .

The best days and times to post are . . .

The tone and content followers benefit from most are . . .

SOCIAL MEDIA *(next year)*

INSTAGRAM

The types of posts followers respond to most are . . .

The best days and times to post are . . .

The tone and content followers benefit from most are . . .

PINTEREST

The types of posts followers respond to most are . . .

The best days and times to post are . . .

The tone and content followers benefit from most are . . .

YOUTUBE

The types of posts subscribers respond to most are . . .

The best days and times to post are . . .

The tone and content subscribers benefit from most are . . .

"SAY YES AND YOU'LL FIGURE IT OUT AFTERWARD"

- TINA FEY

PAGES

When was the last time you went through the static pages on your site? Probably been a while, huh? Review each page making sure you're providing information that shares your message, offers value, and prompts users to action.

Page:

Purpose:

Benefit to readers:

Edits / updates:

Page:

Purpose:

Benefit to readers:

Edits / updates:

Page:

Purpose:

Benefit to readers:

Edits / updates:

MORE PAGES . . .

Page:

Purpose:

Benefit to readers:

Edits / updates:

- -

Page:

Purpose:

Benefit to readers:

Edits / updates:

- -

Page:

Purpose:

Benefit to readers:

Edits / updates:

- -

ADDITIONAL PAGE IDEAS:

PROJECTS + PRODUCTS

Now we're going to cover blog features, series, events, projects, and products—basically anything that was larger than a single blog post and took time to plan, create, and launch. Below, do a little brainstorming on what you'd like to create over the next year, and then on the following pages, evaluate recent products and projects, so your new ideas go off without a hitch! Consider your time and financial investment vs. the return (income, exposure, connections, positive vibes), the plan and process of creation, what worked well and what you would have done differently.

PROJECT:

TIMELINE + PROCESS
(start date, planning, creation, launch)

- -

RESULTS

- -

WHAT WORKED WELL

- -

WHAT I WOULD HAVE DONE DIFFERENTLY

- -

PROJECT:

TIMELINE + PROCESS
(start date, planning, creation, launch)

RESULTS

WHAT WORKED WELL

GETTING SHIT
DONE IS THE
BEST WAY
TO PREDICT
THE FUTURE

WHAT I WOULD HAVE DONE DIFFERENTLY

PROJECT:

PROJECT:

TIMELINE + PROCESS
(start date, planning, creation, launch)

RESULTS

WHAT WORKED WELL

WHAT I WOULD HAVE DONE DIFFERENTLY

PRODUCT:

TIMELINE + PROCESS
(start date, planning, creation, launch)

RESULTS

WHAT WORKED WELL

WHAT I WOULD HAVE DONE DIFFERENTLY

PRODUCT:

TIMELINE + PROCESS
(start date, planning, creation, launch)

RESULTS

WHAT WORKED WELL

WHAT I WOULD HAVE DONE DIFFERENTLY

PRODUCT:

TIMELINE + PROCESS
(start date, planning, creation, launch)

RESULTS

WHAT WORKED WELL

WHAT I WOULD HAVE DONE DIFFERENTLY

EMAIL NEWSLETTER

Sending out a monthly or weekly email to your subscribers? Let's make sure that ish is so good they tell all their friends to sign up too! Use the following pages to evaluate your most-opened emails and figure out why they received all that attention.

Subscribers prefer emails with this type of information . . .

Subscribers open more emails on this day of the week . . .

Subscribers click this type of link most often . . .

Three things I can add to my emails to generate more clicks . . .

1.

2.

3.

Three ways I can gain more subscribers . . .

1.

2.

3.

EMAIL . . .

Subject line:

Day + time:

Content details:

Number of opens: *Number of clicks:*

Subject line:

Day + time:

Content details:

Number of opens: *Number of clicks:*

Subject line:

Day + time:

Content details:

Number of opens: *Number of clicks:*

MORE EMAIL . . .

Subject line:

Day + time:

Content details:

Number of opens: *Number of clicks:*

Subject line:

Day + time:

Content details:

Number of opens: *Number of clicks:*

Subject line:

Day + time:

Content details:

Number of opens: *Number of clicks:*

MARKETING + PROMOTION

Did you land any fantastic features this year? Guest post somewhere cool? Or create a successful collaboration? Do tell . . .

Guest post / feature / collaboration:

URL:

Date:

Time spent:

Compensation:

Traffic + social media engagement:

Notes:

Guest post / feature / collaboration:

URL:

Date:

Time spent:

Compensation:

Traffic + social media engagement:

Notes:

Guest post / feature / collaboration:

URL:

Date:

Time spent:

Compensation:

Traffic + social media engagement:

Notes:

MARKETING + PROMOTION . . .

Guest post / feature / collaboration:

URL:

Date:

Time spent:

Compensation:

Traffic + social media engagement:

Notes:

Guest post / feature / collaboration:

URL:

Date:

Time spent:

Compensation:

Traffic + social media engagement:

Notes:

Guest post / feature / collaboration:

URL:

Date:

Time spent:

Compensation:

Traffic + social media engagement:

Notes:

MARKETING + PROMOTION . . .

GUEST POSTING *(next year)*

Next let's generate a list of websites for which you could write a guest post and share your expertise. If you haven't started already, guest posting is a great way to reach out to readers in your niche that you haven't had contact with or readers in a different niche that may benefit from what you know.

Blog:

URL:

Post ideas:

Blog:

URL:

Post ideas:

Blog:

URL:

Post ideas:

Blog:

URL:

Post ideas:

"IF I WAITED
FOR PERFECTION
I WOULD NEVER
WRITE A WORD"

- MARGARET ATWOOD

ADVERTISING + SPONSORS

Do any advertising this year? Record where, when, and the return on your investment.

Ad info:

URL:

Date range:

Cost:

Traffic + social media engagement:

Ad info:

URL:

Date range:

Cost:

Traffic + social media engagement:

Ad info:

URL:

Date range:

Cost:

Traffic + social media engagement:

MORE ADVERTISING . . .

Ad info:

URL:

Date range:

Cost:

Traffic + social media engagement:

Ad info:

URL:

Date range:

Cost:

Traffic + social media engagement:

Ad info:

URL:

Date range:

Cost:

Traffic + social media engagement:

NOTES:

EVEN MORE ADVERTISING . . .

Ad info:

URL:

Date range:

Cost:

Traffic + social media engagement:

Ad info:

URL:

Date range:

Cost:

Traffic + social media engagement:

**WHY YOU BLOG
IS JUST AS
IMPORTANT AS
WHAT YOU BLOG**

Ad info:

URL:

Date range:

Cost:

Traffic + social media engagement:

NOTES:

- - - - - - - EVEN MORE ADVERTISING . . . - - - - - - -

ADVERTISING *(next year)*

Eyes on the prize! Create a list of places you're interested in advertising next year . . .

Name	URL	Ad Size / Details	Cost / Month

SPONSOR PACKAGES *(this year)*

Review sponsor packages and collaborations that generated income over the past year.

Package:

Description:

Cost / month: Number purchased:

Notes:

Package:

Description:

Cost / month: Number purchased:

Notes:

Package:

Description:

Cost / month: Number purchased:

Notes:

Package:

Description:

Cost / month: Number purchased:

Notes:

SPONSOR PACKAGES *(next year)*

And if you like, create a brand spankin' new sponsor plan for next year . . .

Package:

Description:

Cost / month:

Notes:

Package:

Description:

Cost / month:

Notes:

Package:

Description:

Cost / month:

Notes:

Package:

Description:

Cost / month:

Notes:

BRAND PARTNERSHIPS . . .

Did you work with any companies this year? Let's review collaborations where you received compensation including reviews, sponsored posts, advertising outside of your normal sponsor packages, events, etc.

Brand:

URL:

Description:

Compensation:

Notes:

REMEMBER WHY YOU STARTED

Brand:

URL:

Description:

Compensation:

Notes:

Brand:

URL:

Description:

Compensation:

Notes:

MORE BRAND PARTNERSHIPS . . .

Brand:

URL:

Description:

Compensation:

Notes:

- -

Brand:

URL:

Description:

Compensation:

Notes:

- -

Brand:

URL:

Description:

Compensation:

Notes:

- -

Brand:

URL:

Description:

Compensation:

Notes:

BRAND PARTNERSHIPS *(next year)*

Time to brainstorm! Create a list of companies you'd like to work with next year . . .

Brand	URL	Partnership Details	Rates

BRANDING + DESIGN

Your design is likely the first introduction readers have to you and your style. Just like tidying the house before company arrives, make sure your blog is putting its best foot forward!

- -

What are the most important things for readers to do/see/know when they arrive on your site?
(Join email list, get sucked into reading content, follow on social media, etc.)

1.

2.

3.

Make sure each of these items are front and center, super obvious, and not crowded by less important stuff!

Where are users clicking most and do these items include the three you wrote above?
(Google Analytics In-Page stats (under Behavior) will help you answer this)

1.

2.

3.

BRANDING + DESIGN . . .

What three words or phrases would you like readers to use to describe your blog?

1.

2.

3.

What changes can you make so your overall design conveys this aesthetic?

BRANDING + DESIGN TIPS . . .

ADD / KEEP THESE THINGS

- Blog intro / short bio
- Your name or a pen name
- Email list opt-in in multiple spots
- High-quality photos
- Social media links
- Links to subscribe via RSS + email
- List of 5 - 10 categories (sidebar)
- List of popular posts (sidebar)
- List of regular blog features (sidebar)
- Headings to break up paragraphs
- Links to related posts (post footer)
- Social media share buttons
- A list of FAQ or most requested posts
- Photos = width of the post space
- A design that shows your style
- Contact information
- Product / service links (nav + sidebar)
- Links or info in the site footer
- Descriptive post titles

FIX / REMOVE THESE THINGS

- Tag / label clouds
- Lists of 20+ categories
- Photos in multiple sizes
- Blurry or crunchy graphics
- Repetitive photos of the same thing
- Email opt-in without a description
- Photos without a credit
- More than four colors
- More than three fonts
- White text on black (metal bands only)
- Script fonts as body text
- Underlined links (opt for different colors)
- Giant paragraphs
- Centered or right-aligned paragraphs
- Ads that are not generating income
- Anything that pops-up immediately
- Auto play video or music
- Blog awards and buttons
- Multiple width ads in the sidebar

"SHE STOOD IN THE STORM AND WHEN THE WIND DID NOT BLOW HER WAY, SHE ADJUSTED HER SAILS"

- ELIZABETH EDWARDS

THE NUMBERS *(this year)*

Keeping track of expenses and building a budget is important whether blogging is your full-time job or just extra income. Expenses can include blog conferences, design services, software (Photoshop, apps) or hardware (a camera or laptop), advertising, fonts and stock photos, etc.

INCOME:

Income source:

Time investment:

Monthly income:

Income source:

Time investment:

Monthly income:

Income source:

Time investment:

Monthly income:

Income source:

Time investment:

Monthly income:

Income source:

Time investment:

Monthly income:

TOTAL INCOME:

EXPENSES:

Item:

Benefit / purpose:

Cost:

Item:

Benefit / purpose:

Cost:

Item:

Benefit / purpose:

Cost:

Item:

Benefit / purpose:

Cost:

Item:

Benefit / purpose:

Cost:

TOTAL EXPENSES:

THE NUMBERS *(next year)*

Now let's get an idea of what you'll earn and spend over the next 12 months. If you're hoping to attend a conference, buy a new computer, or cover your hosting costs, planning for expenses at the beginning of the year is not only important for tax time, but will also help project long-term growth.

INCOME:

Income source:

Time investment:

Monthly income:

Income source:

Time investment:

Monthly income:

Income source:

Time investment:

Monthly income:

Income source:

Time investment:

Monthly income:

Income source:

Time investment:

Monthly income:

TOTAL INCOME:

EXPENSES:

Item:

Benefit / purpose:

Cost:

Item:

Benefit / purpose:

Cost:

Item:

Benefit / purpose:

Cost:

Item:

Benefit / purpose:

Cost:

Item:

Benefit / purpose:

Cost:

TOTAL EXPENSES:

BLOG BRAINSTORM

Congrats—you've won the lottery! Woohoo! What will you do with all that cash? Where will you travel? Who will you work with? What will you create? How many readers/subscribers/social media followers will you gain? Where will you be featured? (Or will you just go for a swim like Scrooge McDuck and then take a nap??) Be creative and think BIG!

DON'T WAIT FOR OPPORTUNITY; CREATE IT

MAKE IT A REALITY . . .

Alright you badass blogger, it's time to move forward with confidence and nail some of those dreams! Don't think I'm going to let you off the hook with just a list—now we need to devise a plan!

What can you do on a daily or weekly basis to start making a few of these things a reality? You may not currently have the money, time, or resources to go full tilt toward your goals, but you can definitely build a foundation and start moving in the right direction! As Zig Ziglar said, "You don't have to be great to start, but you have to start to be great!"

When planning the next 12 months, it's important to focus on both short term (three to six months) and long-term goals (one to three years) to not only keep you excited and focused, but also build your online presence in the process.

Launching only massive projects can be a drag on your business, be a catalyst for burn-out, and keep readers waiting impatiently for your next gem. On the other hand, short term goals can leave you and your readers feeling unfocused and overwhelmed. Burn out and overwhelm are two of the biggest enemies of badass bloggers, so we want to avoid them at all costs!

I highly recommend choosing a set of goals that create a cohesive arc for your blog or business, meaning they connect to bring you or your readers through a process to an ultimate goal.

Also consider working in multiple mediums to keep from getting bored. Maybe start the year with a blog series, then shoot a few videos, followed by an ebook and end with a tangible product. What will bring the biggest benefit to your audience? What are you most excited to work on? What will fill your stomach with the biggest butterflies and force you to be brave?

What are you going to do this year to give you and your blog a leg up, put a smile on the faces of your audience, expand your expertise, and make yourself feel like a rockstar? Have faith—you'll never know if something is a good idea or if you have the skills to accomplish it unless you take a shot!

Choose the items from your brainstorm that provide the biggest benefit for you/ your readers/your blog and, using the following pages, list 10 steps to get started.

SHORT-TERM GOAL:

1.

2.

3.

4.

5.

6.

7.

8.

9.

10.

SHORT-TERM GOAL:

SHORT-TERM GOAL:

1.

2.

3.

4.

5.

6.

7.

8.

9.

10.

SHORT-TERM GOAL:

LONG-TERM GOAL:

1.

....

2.

....

3.

....

4.

....

5.

....

6.

....

7.

....

8.

....

9.

....

10.

LONG-TERM GOAL:

LONG-TERM GOAL:

1.

2.

3.

4.

5.

6.

7.

8.

9.

10.

LONG-TERM GOAL:

CONTENT *(next year)*

Alright! It's time to get down to business and make a plan for that badass blog of yours! I don't know about you, but the mere act of organizing my ideas on paper makes me eager to jump into work!

To get started, use the content and social media worksheets on pages 11, 26, and 27 to review what worked best over the past year. Hold on to the type of content that went off like fireworks and clear out what was only a blip on your readers' radar.

There are many methods for building a year's worth of content, but depending on how much you post and the flow of your life, one option may function better than another. Consider how often you prefer to write and how content flows with launches, services, or advertiser collaborations.

No matter *how* you plan, the intent is to have content, social media, emails, and products prepared in advance. This will not only help you create content consistently, but will also allow you to plan guest posts, sponsor collaborations, products, and events with enough lead time to generate a buzz around what you're launching.

If you're feeling overwhelmed, think of it this way—if you post once a month that's only 12 posts per year. If you post twice a month, that's only 24! You can absolutely accomplish that!

And, of course, even if you used pen, nothing is set in stone. Choosing a direction, even if it changes in a few months, it's far better than stressing over every post and launch.

I've included both monthly and yearly worksheets to help with whichever option you choose!

YOU COULD...

- *Plan each month with a different theme*
- *Plan quarterly themes*
- *Choose three or four topics and write one post per week*
- *Choose a year-long theme and break it into 12 months or four quarters*
- *Plan monthly content around quarterly launches of features or products*
- *Use the monthly planner for your content and quarterly planner for guest posts, products, or a marketing plan*

MONTHLY . . .

JANUARY

FEBRUARY

MARCH

APRIL

MAY

JUNE

JULY

....

AUGUST

....

STOP SAYING
"I WISH" AND
START SAYING
"I WILL"

SEPTEMBER

....

OCTOBER

....

NOVEMBER

....

DECEMBER

....

QUARTERLY . . .

FIRST QUARTER

SECOND QUARTER

THIRD QUARTER

FOURTH QUARTER

QUARTERLY . . .

Creating processes is one of the best ways to juggle multiple projects without dropping the ball. You'll be able to simplify and maybe even remove a few items from your daily to-do list which will leave a lot more time in your busy schedule for writing and creating.

I've devised processes for my blog and business to help save my time and sanity like:

- Setting-up Wordpress to automatically post content to my Facebook and Google+ pages because I've found my time is better spend on Twitter and Instagram

- Using BufferApp.com every Sunday to schedule all of my promotional posts for the coming week

- Creating templates for my blog, Twitter, and Instagram graphics instead of starting from scratch every time

The more items on your list you can automate, simplify, or knock out in bulk, the more time you'll have left to interact with your audience and create high-quality content. Because that's way more fun than spending all your time scheduling and emailing anyway!

Task:

New Process:

Task:

New Process:

Task:

New Process:

Task:

New Process:

Task:

New Process:

Task:

New Process:

TIME TO COMMIT!

Now that you've spent all this time reviewing the past year, brainstorming, setting goals, and creating a plan for success, don't file these worksheets away and lose momentum! You've got too much brilliance to send out into the blogosphere to stop now and your readers need all that great stuff!

You now have the tools and insight to gain traction with more focused content, expand your readership by promoting confidently on social media, create bigger collaborations, boost your blog design, be taken seriously by brands and advertisers, and enjoy the whole process even more.

Remember, it will never be the perfect time, you'll never have enough money saved, and other people have always and will continue to do things that you want to do. Don't let perfection or comparison get in the way of launching something amazing—you're just getting started!

Your final task in *The Badass Blog Planner* is to fill out the following Blog Manifesto and post it somewhere you'll read it every single day. Over your desk, next to the bathroom mirror, on the refrigerator. Hell, make a bunch of copies and wallpaper your house if it will help you knock out your goals!

The only way to get what you want is to make it a daily habit, put one foot in front of the other, and do at least one thing every single day to move yourself forward.

GO THE EXTRA MILE, IT'S NEVER CROWDED

Remember your overall goals and use the stepping stones in this workbook to keep yourself moving. Don't forget, YOU are the captain, the CEO, the leader of your tribe, and it's up to YOU to steer the ship.

Join all the brilliant bloggers creating success this year by using the hashtag #BadassBlogPlan! Connect with other bloggers, share what you're working on, be inspired, and help motivate each other.

Wishing you massive inspiration and a thrilling year online! I can't wait to see what you come up with!

xo Sarah

BADASS BLOG MANIFESTO

I will create content that is . . .

To help my readers . . .

Every day I will . . .

Every week I will . . .

Every month I will . . .

This year I will . . .

ABOUT THE AUTHOR

Sarah Morgan is an award-winning web designer and blogging consultant who thrives on helping creative, passionate people grow their online presence, make the leap from unfulfilling jobs, and be brave in business and in life.

In 2012, Sarah quit her corporate design job to literally run away with the circus and get back to what she loves—working with bloggers and small business owners to help them shine online.

Through her blog XOSarah.com, e-course, and books, Sarah inspires her audience to turn their passion into a job they love and build strong, successful blogs and brands.

Connect with Sarah on social media at @xosarahmorgan!

Made in the USA
Lexington, KY
10 October 2018